Jonathan J. G. Lewin was born in London in 1953 and worked in the Civil Service from 1st September 1975 until retirement on 28th August 2015. Interests include nature, wildlife, land conservation, politics, and history. As far as politics are concerned all philosophies and theories have both qualities and flaws and a mixed system/economy is the best for all.

Jonathan J.G. Lewin

From Wireless Light to Radio One and Two

The Evolution of BBC Radio Programming, 1951-1992

AUSTIN MACAULEY PUBLISHERS®

LONDON • CAMBRIDGE • NEW YORK • SHARJAH

A CIP catalogue record for this title is available from the British Library.

ISBN 9781035828296 (Paperback)
ISBN 9781035828302 (ePub e-book)

www.austinmacauley.com

First Published 2024
Austin Macauley Publishers Ltd®
1 Canada Square
Canary Wharf
London
E14 5AA

Table of Content

Introduction

If one was to travel in time between 1951 and any time post May 1992 and was unaware of the various developments and changes in B.B.C. Radio over that period, one would not be able to see any resemblance between the B.B.C. Light Programme of 1951 and B.B.C. Radios One and Two at any time subsequent to 1992.

The said evolvement between 1951 and 1992 was gradual or piece meal with subsequent developments not in mind as and when any development was implicated. As far as this aspect of B.B.C. radio is concerned, there have never been any opening of new radio stations or closures thereon. The most significant branding change was the change from station names to numbers concurrently with the split into two stations (According to nature of programme) on 30th September 1967 (The B.B.C. Light Programme had two frequencies with one then allocated to B.B.C. Radio One and one to B.B.C. Radio Two).

This subject is considered as opposed to B.B.C. Radio Four as there has been nor real changing in the nature of the station or its programming since 1948, other than the withdrawal of most classical music upon the opening of the B.B.C. Music Service on 22nd March 1965 and change from being known as the B.B.C. Home Service from 30th September 1967. B.B.C Radio Three was three separate stations which shared the same frequency prior to 30th September 1967, without any change in the nature of programmes at any time of day or week until April 1970.

Before considering how the B.B.C. Wireless Light Programme of 1951 evolved into B.B.C. Radio One and B.B.C. Radio Two post 1992, it is essential to:-

1. Consider the history of B.B.C. Radio as a whole.
2. Realise that pop/ rock music (And various terminologies) had never been heard of by anyone anywhere in the United Kingdom in 1951. Although it had existed the United States of America since 1948, it was until 1955 thought of only as a short-term fad among younger people unlikely either to extend outside of that country or last for very long.
3. People generally talked about the wireless until between 1948 and 1970. It was mainly people from ordinary backgrounds between the ages of fourteen and thirty in the United States of America from 1948 and in the United Kingdom from 1955 who started talking about the radio. It was from 1963 that more and more people started talking about the radio until this became universal in 1970. The B.B.C. officially started referring to "the radio" as opposed to "the wireless" from 30th September 1967. For these reasons I have included a chapter on the birth of radio/ wireless technology and the British Broadcasting Corporation, and two subsequent chapters on the

history of pop/rock music and its broadcasting on the radio and television.

The reasons why I chose 1951 and post May 1992 are:

1. Whereas in 1951 only 50% of countries (If that) had public broadcasting systems, by 1992 every country in the world had at least six radio stations.
2. It must be noted that in 1951, the United Kingdom, the United States of America, and a very small number of European countries were very much the exception in that they had more than one public broadcasting radio station, or have had public broadcasting systems of any form for more than twenty five years prior to 1951
3. 1951 was approximately halfway between the end of World War Two (1945) and the awareness of/ importation of pop/rock music in the United Kingdom (Early 1955). It was by 1951 that a number of programmes had become recognised parts of the Light Programme; many programmes of which were axed or moved to Radio Four between the beginning of 1968 and the end of 1975 (Some of which to this day remain recognised parts of Radio Four programming).
4. May 1992 is when Radios One and Two have been since they have been as they are today.

1. The Birth of Radio/Wireless Technology and the British Broadcasting Corporation

The idea of wireless communication or wireless telegraphy by wires through the ground, water, and/or train tracks was first considered in the 1830s.

It was in March 1864 that the Scottish thirty-three-year-old mathematician James Clerk Maxwell showed in mathematical and theoretical form that electromagnetic waves through free space were possible. The thirty-one-year-old German physician Heinrich Rudolf Hertz was able to conclusively prove this possible in an experiment in 1888. It was in 1894 that the twenty-four-year-old Italian inventor Guglielmo Marconi built the first complete and successful wireless telegraphy system. Marconi demonstrated the application of radio in military and marine communications and formed a company for the development and propagation of radio services in 1898. Such systems could only communicate a distance of half a mile initially, which was then thought to be the maximum distance which would ever be possible; but longer distances subsequently became possible.

Marconi opened the world's first purpose-built radio factory in Chelmsford in Essex, United Kingdom in June 1912.

The first public radio broadcast was in the United States of America in June 1912; and the first radio station for public broadcasting opened on 14th October 2020 again in the United States of America. Public broadcasting stations by private enterprises were then formed in different places around the world.

Since the introduction of public broadcasting around the world from October 1920, there have been fears that radio could kill the phonograph record industry and live performances with live audiences. I will add that in the United Kingdom, whereas one in five households owned radio sets in 1931 this had increased to four out of five homes by 1938; and record sales had fallen by 65% over the said period.

There had always been concern that as radio technology developed, people who had access to radio might use it, in a way to interfere with other users, whether intentionally or unintentionally. This concern had been expressed by the police, emergency services, mariners, and the armed forces; and in the case of the police and armed forces to intentionally intercept or block their communications.

It was from 1910 that governments around the world had been introducing regulations and legislation regarding the use of radio broadcasting, and with this the requirement for radio operators and users to have licenses.

As far as public broadcasting was concerned, radio companies around the world could fund the cost of their operations through advertising.

The expansion of public broadcasting had become chaotic within the United States of America, with different operators blocking one another's stations, and the problem of interface with listeners subject to the hearing of two or even three programmes at the same time on the same frequency.

In the early 1920s, John Reith a thirty-three-year-old Scottish engineer was looking westwards towards the U.S.A.'s unregulated commercial radio and eastwards towards the fledgling Soviet Union's rigidly controlled state system, and thought that neither would be acceptable for the United Kingdom. He therefore advocated an independent broadcaster able to educate, inform, and entertain the whole nation, free from either political interference or commercial pressure. He was sufficiently visionary to see the potential of broadcasting. He innovated the idea of a government licence fee of which half would be paid to such a radio enterprise.

By 1922, the United Kingdom had sixty-three wireless societies with over three thousand members, and over the first six months of that year the government had received around one hundred broadcast licence requests.

The British government was anxious to avoid the same chaotic expansion as had been experienced in the United States of America and therefore proposed to issue only one single broadcasting licence to one company to be owned by a consortium of leading wireless manufacturers.

The British Broadcasting Company was therefore formed by such a group of leading wireless manufacturers on 18th October 1922, with the first broadcast on 14th November 1922. John Reith was appointed as the company's general manager on 14th December 1922. The company would be funded by a tax (Generally known as a licence fee) on radio receiving sets, to be set by the government and agreed by Parliament. There were 200,000 licenses in 1923. At the same time, the government imposed a ban on public broadcasting by any other wireless operator and a strict prohibition on advertising.

Subsequent to 1925, the consortium of wireless manufacturers were anxious to leave the loss making company; while John Reith was keen that the British Broadcasting Company would be seen as a public service rather than as a commercial enterprise. He favoured the continuation of the unified broadcasting service with its monopoly but realised that more funds would be essential.

John Reith was aware that the government might exercise its right to commandeer the British Broadcasting Company at any time as its "mouthpiece" should that company "step out of line", but anxious to maintain public trust by it appearing to act independently. The government trusted Reith and granted the British Broadcasting Company sufficient leeway to pursue its objectives in the manner of its choosing.

The government issued the British Broadcasting Company with a Royal Charter; and it has been known as the British Broadcasting Corporation since 1st January 1927.

1. The licence and its conditions, and agreement to govern its activities under the Royal Charter, would be controlled by the government minister which was responsible for broadcasting matters.
2. The board of governors would be appointed by the Sovereign on the recommendation of the Prime Minister.

3. There would be no paid advertising (As was normal in the United States of America); with all funding to come from a tax on radio receiving sets (The licence). In the United States of America, the various advertising interests were able to control the radio stations, what would be broadcast at any time, what could be advertised, and when; a system which was not welcome in the United Kingdom.

John Reith was appointed as its first director general on 1st January 1927. He effectively censored anything which he felt might be harmful, whether directly or indirectly.

On 5th March 1928, the government maintained the censorship of editorial opinions on public policy; but allowed the British Broadcasting Corporation to address matters of religious, political or religious controversy. Throughout the 1930s, political broadcasts were closely monitored by the government.

There were 2,500,000 licenses in 1928.

Sir John Reith, as he had become known, had left a legacy of cultural influence across the United Kingdom when he left the British Broadcasting Corporation in 1938.

There was concern throughout Africa, Asia, Australia, and Europe that different countries and radio operators might want to transmit on the same frequencies. It was therefore agreed that radio frequencies would be allocated to different countries under the 1948 Geneva Convention with governments responsible for allocate frequencies to different radio operators within their countries.

It must be noted that in 1951, less than 50% of countries around the world had any public broadcasting networks what ever. Also that the United Kingdom, the United States of America, and a small number of European countries were very much the exception in that they had more than one radio station, or any television whatever.

Experimental television broadcasts were started in 1929. Television was initially regarded as an expensive luxury, there were only 344,000 television licenses in 1950, and it remained a luxury until around 1956, but by 1968 it had gradually become a necessity for virtually every household.

The general usage of television by virtually every household in the country, together with the greater use of portable radio sets and radios in cars, brought about the abolition of the radio only licence fee in 1971, with the British Broadcasting Corporation reliant solely upon television licence fees. In 1971 there were sixteen million television licenses, and in 2022 there were twenty six million licenses.

The Conservative government, which favoured a degree of private enterprise, allowed competition to the British Broadcasting Corporation television network in 1955 by means of another public corporation, the Independent Television Authority (Generally known as ITV):-

1. The extension of such competition to the radio was not considered to be appropriate for a number of reasons. The British Broadcasting Corporation was therefore allowed to retain its monopoly with radio.

2. The Independent Television Authority would allow the independent television companies to broadcast on its frequencies at allotted times of the day and week to raise income through advertising. This public corporation issued licences to different television

companies and could regulate what could be broadcast and/or advertised.

3. It was not until 8th October 1973 that this was extended to the radio; with the Independent Television Authority re-named as the Independent Broadcasting Authority.

One important invention over this period was the transistor as a service conductor device to switch electronic signals. The transistor had been invented in December 1947. The first transistor radio was in October 1954 and first car radio in April 1955. Until then, the only known service conductor device to switch electronic signals was the valve. The advantages of transistors over valves have been.

1. In due course significantly less expensive to manufacture than valves.
2. Whereas valves wore out after a while and required replacing, transistors did not.
3. Significantly smaller in size and weight that valves.
4. Whereas valves heated which meant that they had to be apart from each other and therefore required larger sized radio equipment, transistors did mot which meant they could be next to each other and therefore enabled smaller radio equipment.
5. A significantly larger number of transistors than valves could be manufactured at once.
6. Transistors used significantly lower voltage (i.e. Electric or battery power) than transistors.

7. Whereas valves were easily subject to physical damage due to their size, shape and components; transistors were not.

8. Whereas valves did not function until they heated (Could take up to four minutes from when switching the radio set on), transistors would function immediately upon switching the radio set on.

Many people did however continue to use their valve operated wireless sets until they wore out (Or even purchase second hand valve operated wireless sets) until the mid-1970s. It could be said that the change over from valve to transistor operated radio sets by individual people was gradual between October 1954 and the mid-1970s.

Until November 1969, the General Post Office (The G.P.O.) was the government department responsible for broadcasting issues, under its secretary of state known as the Postmaster General. This responsibility was transferred to the Home Secretary in November 1969. Since 2001, the Secretary of State for Culture & Media has been responsible for matters relating to the British Broadcasting Corporation.

In 1974, it was considered necessary to re-allocate radio frequencies between different countries from the allocations under the 1948 Geneva Convention:

1. Although radio had by 1948 been established in the United Kingdom under the British Broadcasting Corporation and in a number of other countries, many countries around the world did not then have a public broadcasting radio network or ones which were rudimentary.

2. Between 1948 and 1974, more and more radio stations were opening around the world, and likewise more and more transmitters. As a result, there was often interface between stations, particularly in the evening. Between 1948 and 1974, more and more people could afford television, which meant that people generally listened to the radio during the day and watched the television in the evening. However, a considerable number of people still listened to the radio in the evening.

3. It was therefore decided that almost all radio frequencies needed to be re-allocated under the Geneva Convention; and that this needed to be undertaken simultaneously throughout Europe, Asia, Africa, and Oceania (Namely Australia and New Zealand). All countries in Europe, Asia, Africa, and Oceania therefore submitted their respective needs in 1974 and 1975.

4. It was therefore decided that the changes would be implemented simultaneously on 23rd November 1978.

By 1992, every nation in the world had at least six radio stations and three television stations.

The wiping/junking of programmes prior to the late 1970's

Prior to the early 1980's radio and television production companies around the world re used or destroyed tapes of programmes once they had been broadcast.

In many cases, excerpts of programmes have been retained, to-gether with a very few editions of the programmes concerned In other instances all editions of programmes prior to the early 1970's have been completely lost - In a very few instances (Very much the exception rather than the rule), all editions of a programme have been permanently retained.

In the United Kingdom, this not only happened with the B.B.C. radio, but also television on both the B.B.C. and I.T.V.

Prior to the 1970's both video and audio formats of programmes were expensive to store and took up substantial amounts of storage space:

1. The technology for present day digital or audio files did not exist then, which meant that large film or recording reels had to be used. The space then required to store thirty minutes of programming can now accommodate 100 hours of programming.

2. There was therefore the incentive to recycle the tapes with new programmes

3. Maintenance of the pre 1970 reels was very expensive and as reels became older and likely to wear out it was necessary to re-record on to a new reel (The running of tapes had to be at the same speed as used for recording.

4. People involved with programmes had royalty rights which meant that a fee had to be paid each time a programme was broadcast. After taking into consideration these fees and the potential interest in repeats of the programmes concerned, it was not considered viable to retain the recording of the programme (i.e. Copyrights).

5. As far as children's programmes were concerned, children generally preferred new as opposed to older programmes, which remains the position to this day.

With the availability of smaller sized and longer lasting tapes from the early 1970's there was a greater incentive to retain older programmes. Also all programmes were recorded in colour. Policy therefore gradually changed.

All programmes throughout the world have been retained since the early 1980's as recordings were smaller in size and easier to maintain (Television as well as radio).

2. A Brief History of B.B.C. Radio

B.B.C. Radio started on 14th November 1922, licensed by the government. It has operated under a Royal Charter since the 1 January 1927. As there was then only one radio station, that stations was known as the B.B.C. Wireless Service.

The B.B.C. World Service was launched as the B.B.C. Empire Service in 1932 to broadcast to around the world, sometimes in the English language, sometimes in the native languages. It subsequently became known as the B.B.C. Overseas Service from 3rd January 1938, and then as the B.B.C. World Service since 1st May 1965. It has always been broadcast on short-wave.

In order to differentiate between the B.B.C. World Service (Under its respective names) and the domestic B.B.C. Wireless Service, the domestic service became known as the B.B.C. Home Service.

During the Second World War, when the B.B.C. Home Service was concentrating on the "doom and gloom of the war" (To include its news broadcasts, method of presentation, nature of debates, religious output and music), there was a significant call for light entertainment, light drama and music on the radio for the benefit of members of the armed forces.

The B.B.C. Forces Programme (Also known as the General Forces Programme) was therefore opened. It was popular not only among the armed forces, but also among the civilian population as a whole.

At the end of the war in 1945, the concept of the B.B.C. Forces Programme was considered to be so popular that it was decided to make it permanent. The B.B.C. Wireless Light Programme was therefore launched on 29th July 1945 to take on light entertainment, light drama, quiz shows, sport, and music. This left the B.B.C. Home Service able to concentrate on news, current affairs, debates, lectures, serious religious worship, serious religious discussion, heavy drama and serious music.

The B.B.C. launched its Third Programme on 29th September 1946 which had an emphasis on the arts, culture and education. It was only allowed to operate in the evenings for a maximum of twenty-four hours each week.

As a result of the 1948 Geneva Convention on radio frequency allocation around the world, a number of such frequencies were allocated to the British government. The government therefore allocated a number of radio frequencies to the British Broadcasting Corporation, for it to allocate to its then stations, namely the B.B.C. Home Service, the B.B.C. Light Programme, the B.B.C. Third Programme, and the B.B.C. Overseas Service (As the B.B.C. World Service had been known until 1965).

The technology for Very High Frequency (V.H.F.) became available in 1955. Three frequencies were allocated to the British Broadcasting Corporation on 2nd May 1955, which meant that it could allocate one frequency to each of its three domestic stations.

When pop/rock music was imported into the United Kingdom from the United States of America in September 1955, the most appropriate station for this music was the B.B.C. Light Programme.

The policies regarding amount of sport available on the B.B.C. Light Programme was considered to be unsatisfactory for everyone, no matter ones views on or interest in sport:-

1. Some people considered the sport output to be too low while others considered it to be excessive.
2. The B.B.C. therefore launched its Sports Service on Saturday and Bank Holiday afternoons (Other than Christmas Day, Good Friday, and Sundays) on 25th April 1964, to broadcast on the same frequencies as the Third Programme.
3. As a result, people who liked and were interested in sport could have continuous sport on Saturday and Bank Holiday afternoons, while other types of programmes could then be made available on the B.B.C. Light Programme for people who were not interested in sport.
4. However, the B.B.C, Wireless Light Programme remained wholly responsible for radio sports coverage other than Saturday or Bank Holiday afternoons, and also when there were two sporting events of exceptional interest at the same time on Saturday or Bank Holiday afternoons (very much the exception as opposed to the rule).

Classical and religious music, its serious appreciation, and serious discussion about the music, had always been a part of the programming of the B.B.C. Home Service since 1922. Classical music of a lighter nature had often been played on the B.B.C. Wireless Light Programme since its opening in 1945 but was limited to programmes with a mixture of types of music without discussion or comment on the music concerned. There were calls for a dedicated station to provide for this type of music, its appreciation and discussion. The B.B.C. Music Programme was therefore launched on 22nd March 1965 to broadcast on the same frequencies as the Third Programme and Sports Service; 7.00am to 18.30pm weekdays except Bank Holidays; 8.00am to 12.30pm Saturdays and Bank Holidays, and 8.00am to 17.00pm on Sundays, Good Friday and Christmas Day. On this station was offered a more serious appreciation of this type of music, in essence religious and classical music, and was also offered was a considerable amount of speech (i.e., Discussion on the music, musicians, composers, and circumstances surrounding the music).

This, therefore, meant that there were three B.B.C. radio stations, which broadcast on the same frequencies at different times of the day between 22nd March 1965 and 29th September 1967; namely the Third Programme (The arts, culture, and education) to operate in the evenings, the B.B.C. Sports Service to operate on Saturday and Bank Holiday afternoons (Except Good Friday, Christmas Day and Sundays), and the B.B.C. Music Programme (Classical and religious music, its study, analysis and appreciation) to operate from 7.00am in the morning when neither of the two other stations were operating.

On 30th September 1967: -

1. The domestic radio national stations became known by numbers.
2. 2. The B.B.C. Light Programme was split into two stations, Radio One for pop/rock music and Radio Two for all other types of programmes on the Light Programme before then. Its V.H.F. (Very High Frequency) frequency became a part of Radio Two.
3. The B.B.C. Third Programme, the B.B.C. Sports Service, and the B.B.C. Music Programme were amalgamated into a single station known as B.B.C. Radio Three; without changing the natures of programmes at any time of the day week (Until 4th April 1970).
4. B.B.C. Home Service became known as B.B.C. Radio Four. (There were no changes to the B.B.C. World Service, as it had been known since 1st May 1965).

From April 1970,

1. The Saturday and the Bank Holiday afternoon sports coverage was re-allocated to B.B.C. Radio Two; as there was a noticeable call for classical music on B.B.C. Radio Three while the Radio Two audience was low at such times.
2. Radio Three operated as if a single station without compartments.
3. The Radio Two V.H.F. frequency was re-allocated Radio One for a part of the time; namely on Saturday

and Bank Holiday afternoons as V.H.F. was of no benefit to sports coverage, and as and when Radio One broadcast in the evenings between 19.30pm and mid night again as V.H.F. was of no benefit to the then Radio Two programmes.

There were no broadcasting licenses for radio anywhere in the United Kingdom, other than that as were held by the British Broadcasting Corporation, until 1973.

Upon the re-allocation of frequencies around the world with some different frequencies (But not all) allocated to the British government from 23rd November 1978, the B.B.C. therefore decided:

1. To re-allocate 1500 metres to Radio Four (Formerly Radio Two) as it could be picked up in 98% of the country during the day and 83% in the evenings.
2. Radio One to be allocated its own V.H.F. frequency
3. To re allocate Radio One to a better frequency and coverage, as it was the most popular station.
4. To re allocate Radio Two from 1500 metres to two other frequencies.
5. To re allocate Radio Three to 247 metres (Formerly Radio One) as it had a lower audience then other stations and could be picked up by 87% of the country during the day and 38% in the evening.

As Radio One was allocated its own V.H.F. frequency on 23rd November 1978 when all of the frequencies were changed on 23rd November 1978. It was therefore possible for the Radio Two V.H.F. frequency to remain with Radio Two at all times permanently.

B.B.C. Radio Five was launched on 27th August 1990 to take on all sports commentary and news. This therefore meant that it was possible for B.B.C. Radio Two to accommodate music programmes (In essence pop/rock music of past years and decades) on Saturday and Bank Holiday afternoons.

A considerable number of further stations have been launched by the British Broadcasting Corporation since 1992.

It must be noted that even though the radio remains popular to this day, significantly more people listened to the radio in 1951 than at any time since 1992 – whereas television was regarded as very much a luxury only available to the wealthiest of people in 1951 with only one channel (available only in black and white), it has become a basic necessity with numerous channels in colour, which was due mainly to the fall in prices. A new colour television set with four channels in 1992 cost 30% of a second hand black and white television set with only one channel in 1951 in real terms; and in 2015 with over 100 colour channels 15% of a 1951 black and white television set with only one channel in real terms.

2.1. The Shipping Forecast on the B.B.C. Radio

This has always been for the benefit of mariners at sea or planning to sail out to sea:-

1. There have been shipping forecasts since 1859, initially transmitted by telegraph.
2. The shipping forecasts have been prepared by the Meteorological Office since 1911. Its availability during the 1914 to 1918 First World War was restricted for obvious reasons.
3. Since 1922, the shipping forecast has been broadcast four times a day on the B.B.C. Radio, with only small changes in timings and formats since then, except that it was not broadcast during the 1939 to 1945 Second World War for obvious reasons.
4. The shipping forecast consists of weather reports and forecasts around the whole of the British coast, and areas of sea in offshore territories within the United Kingdom.
5. The shipping forecast has always been broadcast on 1500 metres since it was allocated to the British Broadcasting Corporation under the 1948 Geneva Convention as the only frequency which could be received clearly at sea around the whole of the United Kingdom irrespective of the time of day or how weather conditions affected radio transmissions, though that frequency was not accessible to a number of inland areas:-

5.1 That frequency had been used by the B.B.C. Light Programme from 1948 when that station was allocated the frequency. This became B.B.C. Radio Two from 30th September 1967.

5.2 This frequency has been allocated to B.B.C. Radio Four since 23rd November 1978.

6. When 1500 metres was one of the Light Programme/ Radio Two frequencies, the shipping forecast was not broadcast on any other frequency; to enable listeners who preferred to listen to the normal programmes otherwise (i.e. Light, military, pop/rock or mixed music) to do so. However, since 1500 metres became a Radio Four frequency from 23rd November 1978, it has been broadcast throughout the Radio Four network; basically as it was considered preferable to re-schedule and re-time the programmes to accommodate the shipping forecast, as opposed to interrupting the programmes for listeners who could only pick up 1,500 metres.

2.2. B.B.C. Radio Sports Coverage

1. This had been on the B.B.C. Light Programme since its launch on 29th July 1945.

2. This proved to be a very unsatisfactory arrangement, as considerable numbers of people wanted a significant increase in radio sports coverage, while there were also considerable numbers of people who wanted such coverage to be substantially curtailed.

3. The B.B.C. therefore launched its Sports Service, to operate on Saturday and Bank Holiday afternoons (Other than Christmas Day, Good Friday and Sundays) on 25th April 1964. It would broadcast on the same frequencies as the Third Programme and post March 1965 the Music Programme from March 1965, as neither of these two stations operated at such times. Sports coverage however had to remain with the B.B.C. Light Programme, other than on Saturday and Bank Holiday afternoons.

4. From 30th September 1967:-

    4.1 All three stations on the frequency were amalgamated for form B.B.C. Radio Three without any changes in the natures of the programmes at any time of the week. Radio Three was very much in three compartments based of the former programming at any time of day or day of the week.

    4.2 Sports coverage on the radio other then on Saturday and Bank Holiday afternoons became part of Radio Two programming.

5. As Radio One did not generally operate after 7.00pm in the evening with the Radio Two programming on its frequency, following the separation of the Light Programme between Radios One and Two from 30th September 1967; it was decided that evening sports coverage would on the Radio One frequency only from February 1968. This enabled Radio Two to continue with its normal evening programming.

6. B.B.C. radio sports coverage on Saturday and bank holiday afternoons (Except Good Friday, Christmas

Day and Sundays) was moved from B.B.C. Radio Three to B.B.C. Radio Two from 4th April 1970. This was as whereas there was a substantial demand from Radio Three listeners for classical music programmes at such times, the numbers of listeners to Radio Two at such times was very low. Radio Four was not considered to be appropriate as its programmes had considerable audiences.

7. With this change, the Radio One programmes were broadcast on the Radio Two V.H.F. frequency at such times. This was because whereas V.H.F. was beneficial to music listeners, it was of no benefit to radio sports coverage.

8. From 23rd November 1978 when B.B.C. Radio One was given its own V.H.F. frequency, the Radio Two sports coverage was also broadcast on the Radio Two V.H.F. frequency.

9. When B.B.C. Radio One regular/daily broadcasting was extended to mid-night daily from 27th January 1979, evening sports coverage was moved to Radio Two itself as the then recognised radio station for radio sports coverage.

10. Since the launch of B.B.C. Radio Five on 27th August 1990, all B.B.C. radio sports coverage has been broadcast on this station.

2.3. B.B.C. Radio Three

1. Initially, it was three separate stations, completely independent of each other, which shared the same frequency at different times of the day and week:-

   1.1 The Third Programme opened 29th September 1946 with an emphasis on the arts, culture and education. It was only allowed to operate in the evenings for a maximum of 24 hours a week.

   1.2 Sports Service opened on 25th April 1964 to operate from 12.30pm to 18.30pm on Saturday and Bank Holiday afternoons; except for Christmas Day, Good Friday and Sundays. This was an improvement for everyone; people interested in sport as they could have a dedicated station on Saturday and Bank Holiday afternoons; and people not interested in sport as other types of programmes could be broadcast on the B.B.C. Light Programme at such times.

   1.3 The B.B.C. Music Programme opened on 22nd March 1965 to operate 7.00am to 18.30pm weekdays except Bank Holidays; 8.00am to 12.30pm Saturdays and Bank Holidays except Good Friday, Christmas Day and Sundays; and 8.00am to 18.30pm on Sundays, Good Friday and Christmas Day. This station offered a more serious appreciation of music in essence religious and classical music (to include talks on music and composers, and circumstances surrounding its creation; as well as the music itself), and therefore freed up the Home Service and the Light Programme for other types of programmes.

2. On 30th September 1967, these three stations amalgamed to form B.B.C. Radio Three. There was however no change in the nature of programming at any time of the day on any day of the week; which meant that Radio Three could be described as a compartmentalised radio station.

3. As there was a greater demand for classical music on Saturday and Bank Holiday afternoons while the Radio Two audience was very low at such times, the sports programming was moved to Radio Two from 4th April 1970. Radio Four was not considered appropriate for the Saturday and Bank Holiday sports coverage as it had a considerably large audience at the time.

4. Also, it could be said that B.B.C. Radio Three had ceased to be "compartmentalised" from 4th April 1970.

2.4. B.B.C. Radio Four

1. It could be said that Radio Four was the first B.B.C. radio station to operate.

2. B.B.C. Radio started on 14th November 1922, licensed by the government. The B.B.C. then only had one station, which was then known as the B.B.C. Wireless Service.

3. World Service was launched in 1932, then known as the B.B.C. Empire Service. The then existing domestic radio station then became known as the B.B.C. Home Service to differentiate it from the then B.B.C. Empire Service.

4. Upon the outbreak of war in September 1939, the nature of radio programming generally became "doom and gloom"; to include the news/current affairs, debate and discussion thereon, dramas and the music (Which became more sombre in tone). The B.B.C. Forces Programme (which was also known as the General Forces Programme) was therefore opened; to take on light entertainment, light drama, quiz shows, sport and lighter natured music.

5. The B.B.C. Forces Programme became very popular, not only among the armed forces but also among the civilian population. It was therefore decided to make it permanent when the war ended in 1945, with the launch of the B.B.C. Light Programme on 29th July 1945. This left the B.B.C. Home Service for news, current affairs, debates, lectures, heavy drama and classical/religious music.

6. The opening of the B.B.C. Music Service on 22nd March 1965 significantly reduced the classical music output.

7. The B.B.C. Home Service has been known as B.B.C. Radio Four since when the B.B.C. changed from names to numbers for its national network from 30th September 1967.

8. Between 1968 and 1975, a considerable number of speech programmes were re-allocated from Radio

Two to Radio Four, many of which remain part of the Radio Four Programming to this day.

<u>Note</u>

There was considerably more music before then since 22nd March 1965:-

a) In the early years of B.B.C. Radio (i.e., Between 1922 and 1939), there was originally only one domestic station which meant that all preferences had to be considered. Also, as there was not continuous programming in earlier years, music helped people check that their radios were properly tuned and electricians ensure radio sets were operating properly.

b) The opening of the B.B.C. Forces Programme shortly after the start of the 1939 war, enabled a greater concentration on news, current affairs, debates, lectures, heavy drama and classical/religious music.

c) As Forces Programme was popular also among the civilian population, it was decided to make it permanent, known as the B.B.C. Light Programme from the end of the war.

d) The opening of the B.B.C. Music Programme on 22nd March 1965 created a separate radio station for classical/serious music and its appreciation.

e) Between early 1968 and late 1975, a considerable number of speech programmes were moved from Radio Two to Radio Four, to enable continuous music on Radio Two.

2.5. The Wiping Junking of Programmes Prior to 1978

Prior to the early 1980s, radio and television production companies around the world re used or destroyed tapes of programmes once they had been broadcast.

In many cases, excerpts of programmes have been retained, together with a very few editions of the programmes concerned. In other instances, all editions of programmes prior to the early 1970s have been completely lost. In a very few instances (very much the exception rather than the rule), all editions of a programme have been permanently retained.

In the United Kingdom, this not only happened with the B.B.C. radio, but also television on both the B.B.C. and I.T.V.

Prior to the 1970s, both video and audio formats of programmes were expensive to store and took up substantial amounts of storage space:-

1. The technology for present day digital or audio files did not exist then, which meant that large film or recording reels had to be used. The space then required to store thirty minutes of programming can now accommodate 100 hours of programming.

2. There was therefore the incentive to recycle the tapes with new programmes.

3. Maintenance of the pre 1970 reels was very expensive and as reels became older and likely to wear out it was necessary to re-record on to a new reel (The running of tapes had to be at the same speed as used for recording).

4. People involved with programmes had royalty rights which meant that a fee had to be paid each time a programme was broadcast. After taking into consideration these fees and the potential interest in repeats of the programmes concerned, it was not considered viable to retain the recording of the programme (i.e. copyrights).
5. As far as children's programmes were concerned, children generally preferred new as opposed to older programmes, which remains the position to this day.

With the availability of smaller sized and longer lasting tapes from the early 1970s there was a greater incentive to retain older programmes all programmes were recorded in colour.) Policy therefore gradually changed.

All programmes throughout the world have been retained since the early 1980s as recordings were smaller in size and easier to maintain (Television as well as radio).

THE JUNKING/WIPING OF B.B.C. RADIO PROGRAMMES PRIOR TO 1978

The position regarding radio broadcasts on the B.B.C. (And also, television on both the B.B.C. and I.T.V.) was the same as elsewhere in the world for the same reasons.

Prior to the early 1970s

In many instances, all editions of programmes made prior to the early 1970s have been lost in their entirety. In other instances, only a few excerpts and/or one or two editions of such programmes have been retained. In a very few instances, all editions of a programme have been retained.

The 1970s prior to 1978

More programmes and excerpts of programmes were retained as recordings the tapes were smaller and therefore occupied less space, and the tapes lasted for considerably longer.

Post 1978

All programmes have been retained since 1978 as more recordings could be stored in the available space and the recordings could be maintained at much less cost.

The replaying of music of past years and decades on the radio has never been a problem because:-

1. The B.B.C. record library has in its possession a copy of every musical recording in existence since 1922.
2. People like to listen to the recordings/music themselves; as opposed to the way in which the music was presented or the programmes which included such music when the music concerned first broadcast on the radio.

PROGRAMMES ON THE FORNER B.B.C. WIRELESS LIGHT PROGRAMME

The Archers – 1st January 1951 (Sunday omnibus from 21st July 1957) and still broadcasting

The programme lasts for fifteen minutes each weekday evening with a sixty-minute-long Sunday omnibus edition –

Only two pre April 1970 Sunday omnibus editions have been retained in full, and only six 1970 and 1978 Sunday omnibus editions, but all editions have been retained since 1978.

<u>Mrs Dales' Diary – 5th January 1948 to 25th April 1969</u>

This programme lasted for fifteen minutes each weekday afternoon and repeated the following repeated the following weekday morning – Only two editions have been retained.

3. The B.B.C. Wireless Light Programme 29th June 1945 to 31st December 1951

By 1951, the B.B.C. Light Programme provided a wide variety of types of programmes which could be described as "light" in nature. The B.B.C. Home Service could then concentrate on programmes of a more serious nature (e.g. News, current affairs, educational programmes, documentaries, debates, lectures, religion and serious drama.

The B.B.C. Light Programme had been launched as a domestic radio station on 29th July 1945 to replace the B.B.C. Forces (General Forces) Programme as that station had proved to be popular during the 1939 to 1945 war, not only among the armed forces, but also among the civilian population. As with the programming of the B.B.C. Forces Programme during the war, this radio station accommodated a variety of programmes of a lighter nature; to include light entertainment, music of all types, comedy, quiz shows and radio variety shows; not to forget radio sports coverage. There was also classical music, either of a lighter nature or programmes with a variety of types of music, where the music was played with virtually no talk about the music or its performers.

I repeat that pop/rock music, groups, and dancing were unheard of in the United Kingdom in 1951. It had existed in the United States of America since 1948 but thought of as a fad among younger people which would neither last for long nor ever expand elsewhere.

When radio frequencies were allocated to the United Kingdom under the 1948 Geneva Convention, the radio frequencies allocated to the B.B.C. Light Programme were:-

1. 1,500 metres on the long wave.
2. Also 247 metres on medium wave, which although not as good a frequency did provide for the small parts of the country which could not pick up 1,500 metres.

In 1951, the B.B.C. Light Programme opened daily at 9.00am and closed daily at mid-night; basically no change between when it was launched on 29th July 1945 and 2nd September 1957.

Music programmes on the B.B.C. Wireless Light Programme in 1951 included:

1. Request programmes
2. Recorded music otherwise, whether a variety of types or only one type. Overall, all types of music were given equal consideration.
3. Live music – The vast majority of the music programmes were live.

4. Music programmes with one type only (Whether live or recorded) included military bands, string quartets, theatre/cinema organs (at that time live music on an organ was the norm before and between films and theatre performances) music on a piano, light classical music and traditional jazz.

5. Music While You Work 10.30am to 1.00am Mondays to Saturdays and 15.45pm to 16.15pm Mondays to Fridays – continuous music for people able to work while listening to music. It was very popular.

6. Housewives Choice Mondays to Saturdays 9.10am to 9.55am (it must be noted that Saturday mornings were part of the working week).

7. Part of the time was given to popular music of the day.

8. Sundays, around Christmas, and around Easter, were all given over to music with a Christian emphasis.

The various 1951 speech programmes which were subsequently allocated to B.B.C. Radio Four between 1968 and 1975 and are still operating as such to this day include Any Questions, the Archers, A Book at Bed Time, Twenty Questions, Woman's Hour and Yesterday in Parliament.

Saturday and Bank Holiday afternoons (Except Good Friday, Christmas Day and Sundays) from 14.15pm to 17.30pm were given over to sport. Fifteen to twenty minutes sometime between 12.15pm and 13.15pm given over to what will be taking place; and a report on what has happened over the day between 17.30pm and 18.00pm. On occasions at other times, in preference to regular programming, was coverage of major sporting events.

Daily news broadcasts included 9.00am to 9.10am, 19.00pm to 19.30pm (Radio Newsreel), 22.00pm to 22.15pm, and 23.55pm to mid-night.

Part of the programme scheduling had a Christian theme, whether speech (To include prayers) or music/singing; particularly on Sundays, around Christmas, and around Easter.

There were quiz shows and comedy programmes at different times of the week. There were also variety shows during the week to include comedy, sketches and live music.

A considerable amount of the programming was orientated towards serving and former members of the armed forces and their families.

Most of the music on the B.B.C. Light Programme was then live

Saturday programming in general included (nb It must be noted that Saturday mornings were still a part of the recognised working and school week in 1951)

9.00am	News
9.10am	Housewives choice - Music requests from listeners
9.55am	Five to Ten -A hymn, a prayer, and a short story
10.00am	Music from a theatre organ
10.30am	Music While You Work
11.00am	Drama
12.00	Yesterday in Parliament (Now a Radio Four programme)
12.15pm	Music*

14.00pm	Sport
18.00pm	Traditional jazz
18.45pm	Help with listener's problems
19.00pm	Radio Newsreel
19.30pm	Various music programmes, each with either only one type of music, or variety of types of music
22.00pm	Popular songs of the day
23.00pm	Record round up
23.55pm	News
12.00	Close

Sunday programming in general included:

9.00am	News
9.10am	Christian music of a lighter nature
9.30am	A military band
10.30am	Family favourites – Music request from listeners
11.30am	People services – A church services
12.00	Music*
13.00pm	Twenty question (Now a part of Radio four programming)
13.30pm	The Billy cotton Band show (variety)
14.00pm	Music*
15.00pm	Music*
16.30pm	Down your way – the programme visit a locality with ten people interviewed and each asked to choose their favourite music.
17.30pm	Comedy
18.00pm	Quiz show

18.30pm	Music*
19.00pm	Radio Newsreel
19.30pm	Classic music
20.30pm	Sunday half hour – A selection of Christian Hymns
21.00pm	Verity show
22.00pm	News
22.15pm	A Christmas message
22.30pm	Music*
23.55pm	News
12.00	Close

Mondays to Fridays

9.00am	News
9.10am	Housewives choice – Music request from listeners
9.55am	Five to Ten – A hymn a prayer and short story
10.00am	Music*
10.30am	Music while you work
11.00am	Mrs Deles Diary
11.15am	Music*
11.45am	The Archers (Until Friday 30th March 1951)
12.00	Music*
13.45pm	Listen with Mother – For children below five
14.00pm	Women's hour (Now part of radio four programming)
15.00pm	Music*
15.30pm	Film review, or a general look at life

15.45pm	Music while you work
16.15pm	Mrs Dales Dairy
16.30pm	Drama or a story
16.45pm	Music*
18.15pm	Comedy
18.45pm	The Archers (from Monday 2nd April 1951)
19.00pm	Radio Newsreel
19.30pm	Comedy
20.00pm	Debates or topical issues Any Question on Friday – Now a Radio four programs
20.45pm	Music*
22.00pm	News
22.15pm	Topic for to-night
22.20pm	Music *
23.00pm	Book at Bedtime (Now part of Radio Four programming)
23.15pm	Classical music
23.55pm	News
12.00	Close

* Music – The music might be live or recorded, one type or a variety of types of music. If one type might be on a piano, classical music, a string quartet, a cinema/theatre organ, a military band, traditional jazz or light orchestral music.

4. B.B.C. Wireless Light Programme 1st January 1952 to 29th September 1967

A number of changes occurred between 1st January 1952 and 29th September 1967. These were to take account of the birth of pop/rock music in 1955, that there was a dedicated sports station (i.e. The B.B.C. Sports Service) to operate Saturday and bank holiday afternoons (Not Good Friday, Christmas Day, nor Sundays) from 25th April 1964, there was a dedicated classical music station from 22nd March 1965, and that there were preferences which had not hitherto been considered.

The programming continued to include entertainment, comedy, quiz shows, drama, sport and also music of a wide variety of natures.

Also on 1,500 metres was the shipping forecast four times a day as the only B.B.C. frequency which could be picked up clearly throughout all British coastal waters throughout the day.

As from Saturday 3rd January 1953, Housewives Choice was replaced with Children's Choice on Saturday mornings, and Housewives Choice was replaced with Family Choice on

Bank Holidays. There were no changes to Housewives Choice between Mondays and Fridays.

Children's Choice was replaced with Children's Favourites from Saturday 2nd January 1954. The presenter always went by the name of Uncle Mac. The majority of requests were children's songs, the music from children's radio and television programmes, military music, the more known pieces of classical music, some traditional jazz and one or two Christian hymns.

Any Answers was introduced from October 1954, for listeners to write in with comments and opinions of the discussions which had taken place on Any Questions the previous week.

The B.B.C. was allocated three V.H.F. frequencies in 1955, one of which was allocated to the B.B.C. Light Programme.

When pop/rock music and rock & roll was first known of in the United Kingdom in 1955, the then most appropriate radio station for this music was the B.B.C. Light Programme. However only a very limited amount of time was given over to this type of music:-

1. Between ninety and 120 minutes dedicated to this type of music each day, whether continuous or at separate times.

2. The various programmes within which all types of music were considered, whether programmes with a variety of types of music or request programmes. During these programmes, pop/rock music was generally limited to one record every thirty to forty minutes.

The Sunday Omnibus edition of the Archers was introduced on 21st July 1957. This was basically a single one-hour edition of what had taken place over the past week.

The Mondays to Saturdays hours of operation were extended 7.00am to mid-night from Monday 2nd September 1957, and then from 6.30am to mid-night from Monday 29th September 1958. There were however no changes on Sunday hours of operation.

Almost all of the speech programmes and programmes orientated towards a particular type of music as in 1951 were retained through to between 1968 and 1975; though often with some changes to the exact timings of such programmes.

As from October 1958, music was broadcast at different times of the day:-

1. Mixed types of music was broadcast in the mornings 6.30am to 9.00am Mondays to Saturdays, early evenings Mondays to Fridays, and daily in the evenings 23.00pm to 23.55pm – with each type of music taken into consideration.

2. Request programmes – Children's Favourites on Saturday mornings 9.00am to 9.55am, Family Favourites Sundays and Christmas Day 12.00 noon to 13.30pm, Housewives Choice weekday mornings 9.00am to 9.55am except bank holidays, and Family Choice bank holiday mornings except Good Friday 9.00am to 9.55am – The policy was to include a variety of types of music on each programme.

3. Music While You Work was broadcast twice a day Mondays to Fridays from 10.30am to 11.00am and 15.30pm to 16.15pm. This remained continuous

music by a particular team of musicians on each programme without commentary or vocalists.

4. Programmes which relate to a particular type of music, some live with or without a studio audience and some recorded. This included ninety minutes to two hours of pop/rock music a day.

Hours of operation were extended to 5.30am (6.55am Sundays) to 2.00am daily from Saturday 29th August 1964. In essence the Monday to Saturday morning programmes with mixed types of music started sixty minutes earlier, likewise daily programmes with mixed types of music from 23.00pm to 23.55pm were extended to 2.00am, and on Sunday mornings there was a five minute Christian based programme (A Hymn, a Prayer, and brief message) at 6.55am and a mix of types of music between 7.00am and 9.00am.

Whereas almost all music was live on music-based programmes in 1951, almost all music on the B.B.C. was recorded in September 1967.

4.1. Programming Circa June 1964 to October 1966

Some idea regarding how the B.B.C Wireless Light Programme had changed between 1951 and the June 1964 to October 1966 period

Almost all (But not all) music programmes had changed to recorded or on record by 1964

News and weather bulletins every hour at half past the hour by April 1964.

Saturday programming in general included

5.30am	Music*
8.55am	Weather forecast
9.00am	Children's Favourites* – music request from children. Presented by Derek McCullogh going by the name of Uncle Mac-Traditional children's song and pop/rock music twice as often as other types
9.55am	Five to Ten – A hymn, a prayer and a short story
10.00am	Saturday club***
12.00	The week in Parliament (Now a Radio four programme)
12.30pm	Music*
13.30pm	Variety
14.00pm	Music***
16.00pm	Military band music
16.45pm	Music **
18.00pm	Traditional jazz**
18.45pm	Help with listener's problems
19.00pm	Radio Newsreel
19.30pm	Various music programmes each with either only one type of music, or variety of types of music **
23.00pm	Music *
2.00am	News
2.05am	Close

Sunday programming in general included:

6.55am	First Day of week – A hymn a prayer and a short story
7.00am	Music*
8.55am	Weather forecast
9.00am	Christian music of a lighter nature **
9.30am	The Archers
10.30am	Easy Beat***
11.30am	People services – A church service
12.00	Family favourites* – Music request from listeners
13.00pm	The Billy Cotton Band Show (Variety)
14.00 pm	Comedy hour
15.00pm	Movie Go Round - Films due to be released
16.00pm	Pick of the Pops***
17.00pm	Sempreni Serenade**
18.00pm	Sing Something Simple**
18.30pm	Quiz show
19.00pm	Radio Newsreel
19.30pm	Classical music **
20.30pm	Sunday Half Hour - A selection of Christian Hymns**
21.00pm	Verity show
22.00pm	News
22.15pm	A Christian message
22.30pm	Music **
23.00pm	Music*
2.00am	News
2.05am	Close

Mondays to Fridays programming in general included:

5.30am	Music*
8.55am	Weather forecast
9.00am	Housewives choice* Music request from listeners
9.55am	Five to Ten – A hymn a prayer and a short story
10.00am	Music **
10.30am	Music while your work**
11.00am	Morning Story
11.15am	Mrs Dales Diary
11. 30am	Music**
12.00	Music***
13.45pm	Listen with mother – For children below five
14.00pm	Women's Hour (now part of Radio Four programming)
15.00pm	Music**
15.30 pm	Music while you work **
16.15pm	Mrs Dales Dairy
16.30pm	Playtime* – Music for younger listeners
17.00pm	Newly pressed***
17.30pm	Roundabout*
18.30pm	Sport Review
18.45pm	The Archers
19.00pm	Radio Newsreel
19.30pm	Comedy
20.15 pm	Debates or topical issues Any Questions on Fridays – Now a Radio Four programme

	Any Answers on Thursdays – Now Radio Four programme
21.00pm	Music **
22.00pm	News
22.15pm	Music**
23.00pm	Music*
2.00am	News
2.05am	Close

Note - Between first Monday in July and last Friday on or before 17th September in 1965, 1966, and 1967 Mondays to Fridays, the normal 1.45pm to 3.30pm programmes were moved to the then B.B.C. Home Service (When normal programmes on the then B.B.C Home Service on vacation) to accommodate pop/rock music programmes.

* Music - All types of music taken into consideration

** Music - May be one type or a variety of types of music, but no pop/rock music - If one type of music might be on a piano, classical music, a string quartet, a cinema/theatre organ, a military band, traditional jazz, or light orchestral music

*** Music - Dedicated pop/rock music programmes

5. A Short History of Pop/Rock Music

I think that this subject needs to be considered as whereas pop music was non-existent in 1951 (Other than to a very limited extent in the United States of America since 1948 with no one able to think that its consideration could extend to any other country in the world), Radios One and Two have been devoted to pop/rock music since May 1992 (One station current pop/rock music and the other the music 1955 to a year or two prior to the broadcast).

Pop/rock music and associated dancing originated in the United States of America in 1948. Until 1955, it was thought that its appeal would be limited to younger people and youth orientated styles within the United States of America, and that such appeal would be short term, as with many other types of music throughout the world throughout history. Such appeal extended to the United Kingdom from September 1955, and subsequently to elsewhere in the world and in subsequent years to other age ranges.

It can be said that Pop Music grew out of light entertainment and easy listening. It has never been "do it yourself" music but has always been professionally produced and packaged.

The term Pop Music has always been used, to differentiate it from Popular Music which has always been taken to mean other types of well-liked music in line with general tastes. It was also to differentiate Pop Music from folk music or traditional jazz.

Pop/rock music has traditionally consisted either of groups with guitars and drums usually with a vocalist, or a singer backed by a traditional orchestra. Over the course of time groups have used other musical instruments and/or had some orchestral backing, and backings for vocalists have been that as associated with the pop/rock group.

Since the mid to late 1950s, pop music has occupied almost all of music charts in the United Kingdom and United States of America, though other types of music have attained high positions on occasions.

What pop/rock music has traditionally consisted of and sometimes developed into (see last but one paragraph) has also always been known as "Rhythm and Blues". This has been to differentiate it from other types of music successful in the charts and therefore often played on chart based pop music programmes, The term "Rhythm and Blues" was often also used to differentiate from the exact styles which such successful artistes changed to over time, or some of the less played tracts of the long playing records of such artistes (which still fell within the definition of Pop Music).

Pop music has been successful as it has been less expensive to make and easier to dance to then other types of music.

Older generations of people in general tried to suppress the appeal of pop music to younger people and were to a great extent more successful within wealthier and "middle class" families; but were unable to suppress the mass appeal and in many cases began to like the music themselves.

Whereas the United States of America had access to enough radio frequencies to be able to allocate some of these to continuous pop/rock music, the British Government did not have any frequencies for this.

Pop/rock music developed at a slower pace in the United Kingdom then in the United States of America.

Prior to the summer of 1963, pop music on the television or on the stage was in what can best be described as a theatre variety show setting with the artistes expected to wear what to this day can best be described as smart office attire o even formal evening wear (i.e. Dinner suites for gentlemen). This very gradually changed from the summer of 1963, spear headed by artistes like the Beatles and the Rolling Stones:

1. There was a rapid change to audiences dancing to the music, and on television "fairly wild" with artistes miming to their records and members of the studio audience particularly girls throwing themselves at the artistes (not possible when the artistes played live instead).
2. Another change was to performances in stadiums (sometimes very large ones) or in open air parks.
3. At not such a great pace but gradually over a four-year period was a change in dress codes and personal preference. The emphasis became and has remained on originality.

I will briefly consider how pop/rock music on the television evolved in the United Kingdom. Unlike the United

States of America with its numerous television frequencies, the United Kingdom only had two frequencies (Three from April 1964, four from November 1982):-

1. Television performances were restricted to as guest artistes in the various variety shows prior to September 1958.

2. The first pop music television programme was "Oh Boy" from September 1958. The title of the programme generally changed once a year if for no other reason to make the programme look new. The settings were always as for theatre variety shows with artistes, presenters and even studio audiences in smart office attire or formal evening wear.

3. Juke Box Jury started from 1 June 1959. A selection of new or almost new releases were played and a panel of four people (Two from the pop music world and two celebrities from elsewhere) then discussed the record voted on whether they predicted it to be a success "A Hit". When there was a tie, a second jury of three people chosen at random from the studio audience were then allowed to vote.

4. Ready Steady Go started from 9th August 1963. This was the first programme to move away from the variety club setting, with instead the studio audience dancing to the music, close ups of the artistes, and the girls able to throw themselves at the artistes. It was rhythm and blues orientated with artistes performing one or more of their records. Another idea, particularly for female vocalists, was for artistes to start their performances by walking down a flight of

stairs. The programme as a whole was considered to be successful.

5. Top of the Pops started from the 1st January 1964, again with a dancing studio audience and close ups of the artistes. People involved in Ready Steady Go were initially concerned about the potential competition, but soon realised the significant difference between the two programmes; unlike Ready Steady Go which was rhythm and blues orientated with many artistes performing more than one of their records, Top of the Pops was chart based with records played because they were successful in the charts though not within the traditional definition of Pop Music (e.g. Frank Sinatra, Bemard Cribbins, Julie Andrews, Ken Dodd and Dean Martin). Also on Top of the Pops were films while records were played, films of the artistes or previous editions super imposed into the edition concerned.

6. The demises of Ready Steady Go and Top of the Pops:-

    6.1 Ready Steady Go – This was rhythm and blues based with artistes playing more than one record; however pop music gradually became more psycadelic from 1966 which did not fit in with the programme's emphasis – Artistes mimed to the music, girls threw themselves at the artistes while they played and some artistes walked while singing (often down a flight of stairs); all which were not really possible when it was subsequently decided that all performances would be live; also a larger studio was required to enable artistes to "set up" and to accommodate a live orchestra.

6.2 Top of the Pops – By 2006 were numerous alternative ways for people to watch the pop artistes which they preferred when and where they wanted to; as opposed to a set evening once a week.

6. The Increase in Demand For More Pop/Rock Music Programmes On the British Radio From July 1963

There was a noticeable increase in the demand for the amount of pop/rock music available on the radio to be increased from July 1963. However, no action was taken by the B.B.C. as no additional frequencies were available to the United Kingdom and most people were satisfied with the B.B.C. programming as it was. All of the programmes on the B.B.C. Light Programmes were popular among listeners in general, and to curtail any of these to accommodate more pop/rock music programmes would have upset many listeners; or likewise to increase the amount of pop/rock music at the expense of other types of music on the programmes with a mix of types of music.

As in July 1963, programmes were dedicated to pop/rock music:

Saturdays Between 10.00am and 12.00 noon

Sundays From 10.30am to 11.30am, and 16.00pm to 17.00pm

Weekdays Between 12.15pm and 13.45pm

There was also pop/rock music from time to time on the music programmes within which all types of music were considered.

Numerous offshore pirate radio stations were launched round the whole of the British coast during the second half of 1963 and first half of 1964, mostly off the southeast coast, to broadcast pop/rock music twenty four hours of the day, 365/6 days of the year, something which was not catered for by the B.B.C. The most remembered of these was Radio Caroline. There was general concern as the frequencies had not been allocated to the United Kingdom under the Geneva Convention in 1948, these stations could interfere with the emergency services and shipping communications, and they could interfere with other recognised radio stations abroad if not in the United Kingdom. The matter was raised in Parliament in May 1964, but no solution seemed available as no other frequencies would be allocated to the United Kingdom, to block the availability of stations continuous pop music would be unpopular within a substantial size of the British population, and to abolish or curtail other types of programmes on the B.B.C. Light Programme would be equally unpopular within the British population.

It was realised that the closure of the pirate radio stations would not only be unpopular with people who liked pop/rock music, but also with people who did not; as there was likely to be pressure to increase the amount of time given to pop/rock music programme on the B.B.C. Light Programme at the expense of other types of programmes.

Radio Luxemburg, had been providing commercial radio stations for different parts of Europe including the United Kingdom since 1933. This was legal although not licensed by the British government, as programmes were transmitted from mainland Europe from where it had licenses to broadcast abroad. Until 1964, a variety of types of programmes were broadcast. As from 1964, it broadcast continuous pop/rock music each evening between 19.00pm and 2.00am; as this was something which was not catered for on any evening by the B.B.C., even though there was substantial demand for this.

With the opening of the B.B.C. Sports Service on 25th April 1964 to operate from 12.30pm to 18.30pm on Saturday and Bank Holiday afternoons (Except for Christmas Day, Good Friday, and Sundays); the B.B.C. Light Programme could allocate these periods of time to pop music, but with short periods of these times allocated to other types of programmes to include other types of music.

As several Monday to Friday programmes on the Home Service took a break between early July and mid-September; it was decided for these periods in 1965, 1966 and 1967 to move the normal 13.45pm to 15.30pm programmes from the Light Programme to the Home Service, and offer pop music on the Light Programme over these periods.

In 1967, the British government felt that it had no alternative but to take action against the pirate radio stations as they were interfering with emergency services shipping communications, and recognised radio stations abroad, if not within the United Kingdom. The government therefore recommended to the B.B.C. that as the Light Programme had two frequencies that station could be split in two with pop/rock music on one of its frequencies and the other types of programmes on the other of its frequencies.

The Marine Offences Act was passed of 14th August 1967 to effectively close these pirate radio stations.

The B.B.C. agreed with the government to split the B.B.C. Light Programmes into two stations. This happened concurrently with the change from names to numbers for the national network and the amalgamation of the three stations which shared a frequency into B.B.C. Radio Three on Saturday 30th September 1967. B.B.C. Radio One on 247 metres would offer continuous pop/rock music, while B.B.C. Radio Two on 1,500 metres would take on all other types of programmes. It was further decided that the V.H.F. frequency would become a part of Radio Two, which left Radio One without a V.H.F. frequency. On both stations, some new programmes were created, while some existing programmes were extended in duration.

As on 29th September 1967, there has still never been any pop/rock music (whether dedicated programmes or programmes with a variety of types of music) at any time on the B.B.C Light Programme:-

Saturdays – Between 18.30pm and 23.00pm

Sundays – Between 9.00am and 10.30am, between 11.30am and 12.00 noon, between 14.00pm and 16.00pm, and between 17.00pm and 23.00pm.

Mondays to Fridays other than bank holidays – Between 10.00am and 12.00 noon, between 13.45pm and 15.30pm (Other than between 3rd July and 17th September), between 15.30pm and 16.30pm, and between 18.45pm and 23.00pm.

Bank holidays Between 18.30pm and 23.00pm

Between 1st January 1967 and 29th September 1967, the average weekly amount of time given to pop/rock music given by the Light Programme over its hours of operation; whether programmes dedicated to this type of music or included within programmes with a mix of types of music; was only

25% (42% if excluding the periods of time as in the last paragraph). Light Programme listeners could, <u>in general,</u> be split into two groups, those who liked and did not like pop music, with many of the non-pop music programmes of strong appeal to the latter.

7. B.B.C. Radio One Since 30th September 1967

Radio One was transmitted on 247 metres with continuous pop/rock music from 30th September 1967. It did not have a V.H.F. frequency as the former Light Programme V*H.F. frequency was attached to Radio Two. It took on all continuous pop music programmes formerly on the B B.C. Light Programme, some of which were extended in duration, together with some new programmes.

At such times that Radio Two was broadcasting but not Radio One, the Radio Two programmes were broadcast on the Radio One frequencies. Radio Two retained the broadcasting hours of the former Light Programme, namely 5.30am (6.55am Sundays) to 2.00am.

Radio One hours of operation prior to 27th January 1979 were:-

1. As from 30th September 1967, Radio One only broadcast from 7.00am (9.00am Sundays) and 19.00pm. The then consensus of opinion that the additional cost of broadcasting outside of this period could not be justified due to insufficient demand earlier in the mornings, and that continuous pop/rock

music was adequately catered for on Radio Luxemburg between 19.00pm and 2.00am.

2. Radio One did not start broadcasting until 8.30am on Saturday mornings from 3rd February 1968. Although Saturday listening audiences were initially high from 7.00am, these listening audiences gradually became fairly low. The same was applied to bank holidays from the 1968 late summer bank holiday (I have taken the initiative of so naming because exceptional in 1968 and 1969 to all other years, this holiday was the first Monday in September as opposed to in August).

3. Radio One opened at 8.06am on Saturdays from 1st April 1972 and 8.30am on Sundays from 8th July 1973.

As Radio Two (The Light Programme before 30th September 1967) had always been responsible for sports coverage when required after 19.00pm and Radio One did not generally broadcast after that time (With the Radio Two programming on this frequency), it was decided live sports coverage after 19.00pm would be broadcast only on the Radio One frequency from 5th February 1968. This included:-

1. The Olympic Games in 1968 (Mexico) & 1976 (Canada).

2. The Football World cup in 1970 (Mexico) & 1978 (Argentina).

3. The Commonwealth Games 1974 (New Zealand) & 1978 (Canada).

As from 4th April 1970, the Radio Two V.H.F frequency was re-allocated to Radio One on Saturday and bank holiday afternoons; which was when Saturday and bank holiday afternoon radio sports coverage was re-allocated to Radio Two. This was as V.H.F. was not of any benefit for sports coverage.

Radio One was streamlined from 1st January 1972:-

1. Records in the top thirty singles charts except ones which had dropped position in the charts from the previous week; with all records played before any record was again played, and the sequence of playing chosen at random.

2. Once in each thirty minute period at intervals not exceeding forty five minutes:-

   2.1 A record from 1955 to two years from date of broadcast, with each year, each time of year, and type of music ever been in the charts given equal consideration.

   2.2 A new release from over the past week.

   2.3 A tract from a record either in the long-playing charts (Which must not be in or ever have been "the A side" in the singles charts) or the "B side" of a singles record.

3. Some specific types of programmes over each week:-

   3.1 A tract from each record in the top twenty long playing charts in ascending order; no record in or which has been in the singles charts was played unless the long-playing record was a compilation of the singles of a particular artiste or a compilation of records recently successful in the singles charts.

3.2 Records from 1955 to two years before the date of broadcast, which could take one of three formats; the top ten or top twenty on the same date in a past year, request programmes or records chosen at random (but with each year, time of year, and type of music given equal consideration)

3.3 The top twenty singles charts in ascending order.

3.4 New releases over the past week.

3.5 Junior Choice on Saturday, Sunday and bank holidays between when Radio One opened and 10.00am. People below eighteen made requests for records, and often for dedications to be read out; whether linked to birthdays, about to enter examinations or competitions, success likewise, or a change in educational establishment (nb Although all singles discs had records on both sides, all discs in the singles charts were referred by the record on the "A" side without reference to the "B" side, it was the "A" side which was almost always played on the radio or at discotheques, and people with the disc generally only played the "A" side. On the occasions that both sides had or were anticipated to have equal appeal, these were known as "Double A records" and both sides were given equal consideration).

Due to the popularity of Radio One, it was given two much better frequencies in order to make it accessible throughout the United Kingdom and also its own V.H.F. frequency. This happened when the radio frequencies were changed on 23rd November 1978. As a result, the Radio Two V.H.F. frequency broadcast the Radio Two programmes (i.e. Sports coverage) on Saturday and bank holiday afternoons.

From time to time between 5th February 1968 and 26th January 1979, Radio One did broadcast at different times between 19.30pm and mid-night, but was never daily nor continuous; in fact never for more than fifteen hours in any one week.

1. There was always fifteen hours of such broadcasting between 2nd October 1971 and 3rd January 1975.

2. Such programmes were of a more serious study or appreciation of pop/rock music as opposed to the playing of records. Programmes might be speech (Talks or interviews) or consideration of a particular type of pop/rock music accompanied by analysis. It was often the playing of a long-playing album with discussion about the music and artistes concerned; or even interviews with such artistes. There were sometimes recordings of live concerts. Also, discussions regarding why particular artistes were or were not successful; the origins, success and subsequent downfall of a particular artiste or type of music; pop/rock music from abroad with analysis; the potentials of artistes or types of pop/rock music; or projected future developments in pop/rock music.

3. There were periods of time when there were no programmes after 19.00pm (e.g. Between 4th January 1975 and 26th September 1976).

4. Coverage of major sporting events (i.e. International events from abroad between 19.00pm and mid-night British Time) was always given priority. One of the effects of the B.B.C. having to make temporary cuts to its programming output in the mid-1970s was cuts to Radio One's operations between 4th January 1975 and 1st April 1977 inclusive. Initially, there were to be no programming after 7.00pm (except when the Radio One frequency was used for post 7.00pm sports coverage) with the post 7.00pm programmes (and their natures) moved to Saturday afternoons between 2.00pm and 7.00pm, and Mondays to Fridays other than bank holidays between 5.00pm and 7.00pm. Changes were made from 6th October 1975 whereby Mondays to Fridays except bank holidays Radio One would close at 6.00pm but re-open 11.00pm to midnight with daytime singles records continuing to closure at 6.00pm and former post 10.00pm programming for sixty minutes 11.00pm to mid night (No changes to weekends or bank holidays).

As from 27th January 1979, Radio One operated from 6.00am (8.00am Sundays) until mid-night. This meant that the 19.00pm to mid night radio sports coverage (When required) had to be returned to Radio Two. Saturday afternoons between 14.00pm and 19.00pm, and Mondays to Fridays between 22.00pm and mid-night were allocated to the programmes as detailed in item three of the previous paragraph.

Between the middle of May 1980 and early in May 1992, the pop/rock music of all past years and decades was gradually re-allocated to Radio Two, which enabled Radio One to concentrate wholly on present day pop/rock music. Junior Choice (Weekends and bank holidays in the 1970s, since 27th January 1979 from 8.00am to 10.00am) was discontinued as a programme early in 1982, though 8.00am to 10.00am weekends and bank holidays remained a time for people below eighteen to make requests until early in 1984. Radio One was also able to orientate towards "teens and twenties" with news summaries presented in a way of general appeal to them, and on occasions people from this age range able to express views and opinions on the news and current affairs.

Radio One has operated for twenty four hours of the day since 1st May 1991.

B.B.C. Radio One Extra was launched on 16th August 2002 with programmes with specific types of pop/rock music (e.g. Caribbean, African, Asian, ethnic minorities, rock, funk, punk, reggae, documentaries about current pop/rock music, pop/rock music concerts past and present and not to forget the programming as detailed in item two of the last but three paragraphs).

One programme which started on the B.B.C. Light Programme in the 1950s, was allocated to Radio One when the Light Programme split on 30th September 1967, and is still operating today, is the Sunday afternoon singles chart rundown; though the title of programme has changed on several occasions and now has a longer duration then when it first started. It started off as the top ten singles, subsequently extended to the top twenty singles from when it became Radio One from 30th September 1967 (Sunday 1st October 1967 to be exact), and the top sixty over a three-hour period from

October 1972. This reverted to the top twenty from 17th March 1974 and people were generally interested in other aspects of pop music as opposed to the lower half of the top sixty. It has remained as the top forty since 12th November 1978.

8. B.B.C. Radio Two
Since 30th September 1967

B.B.C. Radio Two was transmitted on 1500 metres and took on all programmes formerly on the B.B.C. Light Programme, other than the continuous pop music programmes. Some of the programmes which remained with Radio Two were extended in duration, and there were also a number of new programmes. The V.H.F. frequency of the former B.B.C. Light Programme was allocated to this station.

Radio Two broadcast on the radio from 5.30am (6.55am Sundays) to 2.00am, the same as the former B.B.C. Light Programme. The starting time changed to 5.00am Mondays to Saturdays from 1st April 1972. One of the effects of the need to the B.B.C. to make temporary cuts to its programming in the mid-1970s, was that between 4th January 1975 and 31st March 1978 inclusive, Radio Two operated from 6.00am (No change on Sundays) to 12.30am, and Mondays to Fridays except bank holidays closed in the afternoons between 2.00pm and 5.00pm when the Radio One programming was broadcast on the Radio Two frequency. It has broadcast continuously twenty-four hours of the day 365/6 days of the year since 5.00am on 27th January 1979.

1. Between early 1968 and late 1975, Radio Two gradually became a continuous music station with all types of music taken into consideration equally; with all speech programmes either gradually axed or re-allocated to B.B.C. Radio Four. The exceptions to this were:

2. The Shipping Forecast – This remained with Radio Two until 23rd November 1978 as the then Radio Two frequency (1,500 metres) was the only B.B.C. frequency which could be picked up clearly in all British coastal and offshore areas. The Shipping Forecast became part of Radio Four programming from 23rd November 1978 when 1,500 metres was re-allocated to Radio Four (With Radio Two re-allocated two medium wave frequencies).

Radio sports coverage – Radio Four was not considered to be appropriate for radio sports coverage which meant that radio sports coverage other than Saturday and Bank Holiday afternoons (Radio Three and its fore runner since April 1964) remained as a part of the Radio Two Programming – The Saturday and Bank Holiday afternoon sports coverage was also re-allocated to Radio Two on 4th April 1970, as there was substantial demand from Radio Three listeners for classical music to be extended to such times of the week – When B.B.C. Radio Five opened on 27th August 1990 this new station tools on all radio sports coverage, which "freed up" Radio Two for other types of programmes at such times.

Until Radio One had its own V.H.F. frequency from 23rd November 1978:-

1. The Radio Two V.H.F. frequency was re-allocated to Radio One on Saturday and bank holiday afternoons (Other. than Christmas Day, Good Friday and Sundays) from April 1970, as Radio Two was broadcasting sport.

2. As and when Radio One did operate after 7.30pm, the Radio Two V.H.F. frequency was re-allocated to Radio One for around 50% of such times, as the post 7.30pm Radio One programmes (when it was broadcasting) were then offering a more serious appreciation of pop/rock music.

Between the middle of May 1980 and the early May 1992, the pop/rock music of all past years and decades was gradually re-allocated from Radio One to Radio Two, which enabled Radio One to concentrate wholly on present day pop/rock music.

Since the beginning of May 1992, Radio Two has been basically pop/rock music of past years and decades, in essence 1955 to two years before the date of broadcast, as there was a greater demand for this type of music as opposed to other types of music. This has basically consisted of:-

1. The top ten or top twenty on the same date in a past year.
2. Request programmes.
3. The records of a particular decade.
4. Records chosen at random (But with each year, time of year and type of music given equal consideration).
5. Each decade had a weekly programme; the 1950s, 1960s and 1970s from February 1983; the 1980s from

mid-1992; and the 1990s from 2002. Each of these programmes lasted for sixty minutes, which was extended to two hours from January 1992.

The following programmes started off on the B.B.C. Light Programme during the 1950s or late 1940s, were allocated to B.B.C. Radio Two on 30th September 1967, were reallocated to B.B.C. Radio Four between early 1968 and late 1975, and still to this day remain recognised features of B.B.C. Radio Four programming:-

Any Answers

Any Questions

The Archers

Gardener's Question Time.

The weekday morning story

Woman's Hour

Yesterday in Parliament

If one was to say between early 1968 and November 1978, one could add the shipping forecasts.

So it can be said that Radio Two changed considerably over the just under twenty five year period between 30th September 1967 and May 1992. From 30th September 1967, this station consisted of programmes orientated to a pre-1951 type of music, programmes with all types of music considered equally, light dramas, light storytelling, comedy, quiz shows, some religious programmes and sport; with pop/rock music limited to programmes with a mix of types of music where it was played in the same frequencies as other types of music. Since 1992, it has consisted wholly of the pop/rock music of various forms 1955 to two years before the broadcast.

Conclusion

So it can be seen that although the B.B.C. Light Programme of 1951 gradually evolved on a piece meal basis into B.B.C. Radios One and Two post May 1992, a person who travelled in time between 1951 and anytime on or after May 1992 would not be able to see any resemblances.

After all whereas the B.B.C. Light Programmes of 1951 offered light entertainment of various forms to include variety shows and comedy, light dramas, quiz shows, some current affairs and debating programmes, and all types of music as in existence then; to include also a number programmes which since 1975 have been associated with B.B.C. Radio Four (November 1978 if the Shipping Forecast is included) and remain so to this day; both Radios One and Two since 1992 have continuously broadcast types of music which did not exist and people did not think would ever exist in 1951 (other than as a short term "fad" among younger people within the United States of America unlikely to expand, be noticed, or be given any consideration in the United Kingdom or any other nation).

It does really irritate me when people talk about 30th September 1967 as the birth of B.B.C. Radio One. What then really happened was the change from names to numbers for the B.B.C. Radio network, the amalgamation of the three stations which shared a frequency into a single station (namely B.B.C. Radio Three) without any change in the nature of programming at any time of the week or day for over two years, and the split of the B.B.C. Light Programme into two stations with each of these two stations allocated one of its two former frequencies.